Light Cooking™

PASTA

PUBLICATIONS INTERNATIONAL, LTD.

Food Guide Pyramid source: U.S. Department of Agriculture/U.S. Department of Health and Human Services.

Recipe Development: Kathleen German, Food Consultant
Nutritional Analysis: Linda R. Yoakam, M.S., R.D.

Photography: Burke/Triolo Productions, Culver City, CA

Serving dishes on pages 11, 15, 17, 53 and 61 courtesy of Tesoro, Los Angeles, CA.

Pictured on the front cover: Vegetable Lasagna (*page 42*).
Pictured on the inside front cover: Sweet and Sour Broccoli Pasta Salad (*page 18*).
Pictured on the inside back cover: Lemon Tossed Linguine (*page 80*).
Pictured on the back cover (*clockwise from top right*): Grilled Ratatouille (*page 22*), Spicy Lentil and Pasta Soup (*page 34*), Pasta Primavera (*page 56*) and Jamaican Seafood Salad (*page 12*).

ISBN: 0-7853-0793-1

Manufactured in U.S.A.

8 7 6 5 4 3 2 1

Microwave Cooking: Microwave ovens vary in wattage. The microwave cooking times given in this publication are approximate. Use the cooking times as guidelines and check for doneness before adding more time. Consult manufacturer's instructions for suitable microwave-safe cooking dishes.

CONTENTS

11.99

Lessons in Smart Eating _____ 6

Salads _____ 10

Soups _____ 28

Entrees _____ 40

Side Dishes _____ 80

Nutrition Reference Chart _____ 92

Index _____ 93

Metric Chart _____ 94

LESSONS IN SMART EATING

Today, people everywhere are more aware than ever before about the importance of maintaining a healthful lifestyle. In addition to proper exercise, this includes eating foods that are lower in fat, sodium and cholesterol. The goal of *Light Cooking* is to provide today's cook with easy-to-prepare recipes that taste great, yet easily fit into your dietary goals. Eating well is a matter of making smarter choices about the foods you eat. Preparing the recipes in *Light Cooking* is your first step toward making smart choices a delicious reality.

A Balanced Diet

The U.S. Department of Agriculture and the Department of Health and Human Services have developed a Food Guide Pyramid to illustrate how easy it is to eat a healthier diet. It is not a rigid prescription, but rather a general guide that lets you choose a healthful diet that's right for you. It calls for eating a wide variety of foods to get the nutrients you need and, at the same time, the right amount of calories to maintain a healthy weight.

Food Guide Pyramid
A Guide to Daily Food Choices

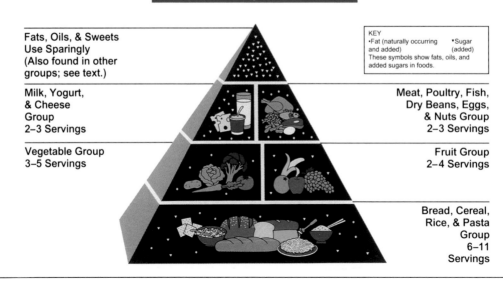

Fats, Oils, & Sweets
Use Sparingly
(Also found in other
groups; see text.)

KEY
•Fat (naturally occurring   ▼Sugar
and added)   (added)
These symbols show fats, oils, and
added sugars in foods.

Milk, Yogurt,
& Cheese
Group
2–3 Servings

Meat, Poultry, Fish,
Dry Beans, Eggs,
& Nuts Group
2–3 Servings

Vegetable Group
3–5 Servings

Fruit Group
2–4 Servings

Bread, Cereal,
Rice, & Pasta
Group
6–11
Servings

The number of servings, and consequently, the number of calories a person can eat each day, is determined by a number of factors, including age, weight, height, activity level and gender. Sedentary women and some older adults need about 1,600 calories each day. For most children, teenage girls, active women and many sedentary men 2,000 calories is about right. Teenage boys, active men and some very active women use about 2,800 calories each day. Use the chart below to determine how many servings you need for your calorie level.

Personalized Food Group Servings for Different Calorie Levels*			
	1,600	2,000	2,800
Bread Group Servings	6	8	11
Vegetable Group Servings	3	4	5
Fruit Group Servings	2	3	4
Milk Group Servings	2–3**	2–3**	2–3**
Meat Group Servings (ounces)	5	6	7

* Numbers may be rounded.
** Women who are pregnant or breast-feeding, teenagers and young adults to age 24 need 3 or more servings.

Lower Fat for Healthier Living

It is widely known that most Americans' diets are too high in fat. A low fat diet reduces your risk of getting certain diseases and helps you maintain a healthy weight. Studies have shown that eating more than the recommended amount of fat (especially saturated fat) is associated with increased blood cholesterol levels in some adults. A high blood cholesterol level is associated with increased risk for heart disease. A high fat diet may also increase your chances for obesity and some types of cancer.

Nutrition experts recommend diets that contain 30% or less of total daily calories from fat. The "30% calories from fat" goal applies to a total diet over time, not to a single food, serving of a recipe or meal. To find the approximate percentage of calories from fat use this easy 3-step process: ·

1 Multiply the grams of fat per serving by 9 (there are 9 calories in each gram of fat), to give you the number of calories from fat per serving.

2 Divide by the total number of calories per serving.

3 Multiply by 100%.

For example, imagine a 200 calorie sandwich that has 10 grams of fat.
To find the percentage of calories from fat, first multiply the grams of fat by 9: $10 \times 9 = 90$

Then, divide by the total number of calories in a serving: $90 \div 200 = .45$

Multiply by 100% to get the percentage of calories from fat: $45 \times 100\% = 45\%$

You may find doing all this math tiresome, so an easier way to keep track of the fat in your diet is to calculate the total *grams* of fat appropriate to your caloric intake, then keep a running count of fat grams over the course of a day. The Nutrition Reference Chart on page 92 lists recommended daily fat intakes based on calorie level.

Defining "Fat Free"

It is important to take the time to read food labels carefully. For example, you'll find many food products on the grocery store shelves making claims such as "97% fat free." This does not necessarily mean that 97% of the *calories* are free from fat (or that only 3 percent of calories come from fat). Often these numbers are calculated by weight. This means that out of 100 grams of this food, 3 grams are fat. Depending on what else is in the food, the percentage of calories from fat can be quite high. You may find that the percent of calories *from fat* can be as high as 50%.

Daily Values

Fat has become the focus of many diets and eating plans. This is because most Americans' diets are too high in fat. However, there are other important nutrients to be aware of, including saturated fat, sodium, cholesterol, protein, carbohydrates and several vitamins and minerals. Daily values for these nutrients have been established by the government and reflect current nutritional recommendations for a 2,000 calorie reference diet. They are appropriate for most adults and children (age 4 or older) and provide excellent guidelines for an overall healthy diet. The chart on page 92 gives the daily values for 11 different items.

Nutritional Analysis

Every recipe in *Light Cooking* is followed by a nutritional analysis block that lists certain nutrient values for a single serving.

■   The analysis of each recipe includes all the ingredients that are listed in that recipe, *except* ingredients labeled as "optional" or "for garnish."

■   If a range is given in the yield of a recipe ("Makes 6 to 8 servings" for example), the *lower* yield was used to calculate the per serving information.

■ If a range is offered for an ingredient ("¼ to ⅛ teaspoon" for example), the *first* amount given was used to calculate the nutrition information.

■ If an ingredient is presented with an option ("2 cups hot cooked rice or noodles" for example), the *first* item listed was used to calculate the nutritional information.

■ Foods shown in photographs on the same serving plate and offered as "serve with" suggestions at the end of a recipe are *not* included in the recipe analysis unless they are listed in the ingredient list.

■ Meat should be trimmed of all visible fat since this is reflected in the nutritional analysis.

■ In recipes calling for cooked rice or noodles, the analysis was based on rice or noodles that were prepared without added salt or fat unless otherwise mentioned in the recipe.

The nutrition information that appears with each recipe was calculated by an independent nutrition consulting firm. Every effort has been made to check the accuracy of these numbers. However, because numerous variables account for a wide range of values in certain foods, all analyses that appear in this book should be considered approximate.

The recipes in this publication are *not* intended as a medically therapeutic program, nor as a substitute for medically approved diet plans for people on fat, cholesterol or sodium restricted diets. You should consult your physician before beginning any diet plan. The recipes offered here can be a part of a healthy lifestyle that meets recognized dietary guidelines. A healthy lifestyle includes not only eating a balanced diet, but engaging in proper exercise as well.

All the ingredients called for in these recipes are generally available in large supermarkets, so there is no need to go to specialty or health food stores. You'll also see an ever-increasing amount of reduced fat and nonfat products available in local markets. Take advantage of these items to reduce your daily fat intake even more.

Cooking Healthier

When cooking great-tasting low fat meals, you will find some techniques or ingredients are different from traditional cooking. Fat serves as a flavor enhancer and gives foods a distinctive and desirable texture. In order to compensate for the lack of fat and still give great-tasting results, many of the *Light Cooking* recipes call for a selection of herbs or a combination of fresh vegetables. A wide variety of grains and pastas are also used. Many of the recipes call for alternative protein sources, such as dried beans or tofu. Often meat is included in a recipe as an accent flavor rather than the star attraction. Vegetables are often "sautéed" in a small amount of broth rather than oil. Applesauce may be added to baked goods to give a texture similar to full fat foods. These are all simple changes that you can easily make when you start cooking healthy!

Salads

SALMON AND GREEN BEAN SALAD WITH PASTA

All salmon are high in protein, the B vitamins, vitamin A and are also a rich source of OMEGA-3 oils, which studies show protect against heart disease.

Nutrients per Serving:

Calories	210
(15% of calories from fat)	
Total Fat	3 g
Saturated Fat	1 g
Cholesterol	15 mg
Sodium	223 mg
Carbohydrate	29 g
Dietary Fiber	2 g
Protein	16 g
Calcium	118 mg
Iron	2 mg
Vitamin A	383 RE
Vitamin C	5 mg

DIETARY EXCHANGES:
1½ Starch/Bread, 1½ Lean Meat, ½ Vegetable

1 can (6¼ ounces) salmon
8 ounces uncooked small whole wheat or regular pasta shells
¾ cup fresh green beans, cut into 2-inch pieces
⅔ cup finely chopped carrots
½ cup nonfat cottage cheese
3 tablespoons plain nonfat yogurt
1½ tablespoons lemon juice
1 tablespoon fresh dill
2 teaspoons grated onion
1 teaspoon prepared mustard

1 Drain salmon and separate into chunks; set aside.

2 Cook pasta according to package directions, including ¼ teaspoon salt; add green beans during last 3 minutes of cooking. Drain and rinse well under cold water until pasta and green beans are cool.

3 Combine pasta, green beans, carrots and salmon in medium bowl.

4 Place cottage cheese, yogurt, lemon juice, dill, onion and mustard in blender or food processor; process until smooth. Pour over pasta mixture; toss to coat evenly. Garnish as desired.

Makes 6 (1-cup) servings

JAMAICAN SEAFOOD SALAD

You can almost feel the tropical breezes as you savor each bite of this delicate seafood and pasta salad.

Nutrients per Serving:

Calories	136
(15% of calories from fat)	
Total Fat	3 g
Saturated Fat	<1 g
Cholesterol	56 mg
Sodium	269 mg
Carbohydrate	19 g
Dietary Fiber	1 g
Protein	9 g
Calcium	54 mg
Iron	2 mg
Vitamin A	36 RE
Vitamin C	7 mg

DIETARY EXCHANGES:
1 Starch/Bread, 1 Lean Meat, ½ Vegetable

6 ounces uncooked vermicelli noodles
6 ounces fresh or imitation crabmeat
4 ounces cooked medium shrimp
1 cup diagonally sliced yellow squash
1 cup diagonally sliced zucchini
1 tablespoon rice wine vinegar
1 tablespoon reduced sodium soy sauce
1 tablespoon minced fresh cilantro
1 tablespoon lime juice
2 teaspoons Oriental sesame oil
2 teaspoons grated fresh ginger
1 teaspoon grated lime peel
⅛ teaspoon ground cinnamon

1 Cook noodles according to package directions, omitting salt. Drain and rinse well under cold water until pasta is cool; drain well.

2 Combine crabmeat, shrimp, yellow squash and zucchini in medium bowl.

3 Combine vinegar, soy sauce, cilantro, lime juice, sesame oil, ginger, lime peel and cinnamon in small bowl; pour over vegetable mixture.

4 Toss to coat evenly. Serve over noodles, chilled or at room temperature.

Makes 6 (1-cup) servings

GAZPACHO MACARONI SALAD

Gazpacho is traditionally an uncooked soup of puréed fresh vegetables. Here we have chopped the vegetables and mixed them with macaroni; the result—a healthy and colorful array for all your senses.

Nutrients per Serving:

Calories	136
(11% of calories from fat)	
Total Fat	2 g
Saturated Fat	<1 g
Cholesterol	0 mg
Sodium	114 mg
Carbohydrate	27 g
Dietary Fiber	3 g
Protein	5 g
Calcium	33 mg
Iron	2 mg
Vitamin A	91 RE
Vitamin C	56 mg

DIETARY EXCHANGES:
1 Starch/Bread, ½ Fat,
2½ Vegetable

4 ounces uncooked macaroni
2½ cups chopped, seeded tomatoes
1 cup finely chopped red onion
1 cup finely chopped cucumber
½ cup finely chopped celery
½ cup finely chopped green bell pepper
½ cup finely chopped red bell pepper
3 tablespoons cider vinegar
2 tablespoons finely chopped black olives
1 bay leaf
2 tablespoons minced fresh parsley *or* 1 teaspoon dried parsley
1 tablespoon fresh thyme *or* ½ teaspoon dried thyme leaves
1 clove garlic, minced
3 to 4 dashes hot pepper sauce
¼ teaspoon ground black pepper

1 Cook pasta according to package directions, omitting salt. Drain and rinse well under cold water until pasta is cool; drain well.

2 Combine pasta and remaining ingredients in medium bowl. Cover and refrigerate 4 hours for flavors to blend. Remove bay leaf before serving. Garnish with whole olives, cucumber slices and dill sprigs, if desired. Serve chilled or at room temperature.

Makes 6 (1-cup) servings

CHICKEN CAESAR SALAD

Indulge yourself in this guilt-free Caesar salad, using low fat ingredients to duplicate the flavors of the high fat original.

Nutrients per Serving:

Calories	379
(19% of calories from fat)	
Total Fat	8 g
Saturated Fat	2 g
Cholesterol	56 mg
Sodium	294 mg
Carbohydrate	45 g
Dietary Fiber	7 g
Protein	32 g
Calcium	171 mg
Iron	4 mg
Vitamin A	339 RE
Vitamin C	35 mg

DIETARY EXCHANGES:
2 Starch/Bread, 3 Lean
Meat, 3 Vegetable

4 small boneless skinless chicken breast halves
6 ounces uncooked gnocchi or other dried pasta
1 package (9 ounces) frozen artichoke hearts, thawed
1½ cups cherry tomatoes, quartered
¼ cup plus 2 tablespoons plain nonfat yogurt
2 tablespoons reduced calorie mayonnaise
2 tablespoons grated Romano cheese
1 tablespoon sherry or red wine vinegar
1 clove garlic, minced
½ teaspoon anchovy paste
½ teaspoon Dijon mustard
½ teaspoon ground white pepper
1 small head romaine lettuce, torn into bite-size pieces
1 cup toasted bread cubes

1 Grill or broil chicken breasts until no longer pink in center; set aside.

2 Cook pasta according to package directions, omitting salt. Drain and rinse well under cold water until pasta is cool; drain well. Combine pasta, artichoke hearts and tomatoes in large bowl; set aside.

3 Combine yogurt, mayonnaise, Romano cheese, sherry, garlic, anchovy paste, mustard and white pepper in small bowl; whisk until smooth. Add to pasta mixture; toss to coat evenly.

4 Arrange lettuce on platter or individual plates. Spoon pasta mixture over lettuce. Thinly slice chicken breasts and place on top of pasta. Sprinkle with bread cubes.

Makes 4 main-dish servings

SWEET AND SOUR BROCCOLI PASTA SALAD

If you have shied away from sweet and sour dishes because of the high fat content, then this dish is for you! Apple juice, cider vinegar, mustard, honey and nonfat yogurt provide the taste sensations in this nutritious salad.

Nutrients per Serving:

Calories	198
(15% of calories from fat)	
Total Fat	3 g
Saturated Fat	1 g
Cholesterol	<1 mg
Sodium	57 mg
Carbohydrate	36 g
Dietary Fiber	3 g
Protein	7 g
Calcium	55 mg
Iron	2 mg
Vitamin A	389 RE
Vitamin C	31 mg

DIETARY EXCHANGES:
2 Starch/Bread, ½ Fruit,
½ Vegetable, ½ Fat

8 ounces uncooked pasta twists
2 cups broccoli florets
⅔ cup shredded carrots
1 medium Red or Golden Delicious apple, cored, seeded and chopped
⅓ cup plain nonfat yogurt
⅓ cup apple juice
3 tablespoons cider vinegar
1 tablespoon light olive oil
1 tablespoon Dijon mustard
1 teaspoon honey
½ teaspoon dried thyme leaves
   Lettuce leaves

1 Cook pasta according to package directions, omitting salt and adding broccoli during the last 2 minutes. Drain and rinse well under cold water until pasta and broccoli are cool; drain well.

2 Place pasta, broccoli, carrots and apple in medium bowl.

3 Combine yogurt, apple juice, cider vinegar, oil, mustard, honey and thyme in small bowl. Pour over pasta mixture; toss to coat evenly.

4 Serve on individual dishes lined with lettuce. Garnish with apple slices, if desired.

Makes 6 (1-cup) servings

SMOKED TURKEY PASTA SALAD

This simple and fast pasta salad can be prepared in advance and refrigerated until you are ready to serve. The smoked turkey gives this salad an imaginative flair.

Nutrients per Serving:

Calories	233
(19% of calories from fat)	
Total Fat	5 g
Saturated Fat	1 g
Cholesterol	12 mg
Sodium	249 mg
Carbohydrate	34 g
Dietary Fiber	5 g
Protein	13 g
Calcium	34 mg
Iron	2 mg
Vitamin A	12 RE
Vitamin C	4 mg

DIETARY EXCHANGES:
2 Starch/Bread, 1 Lean
Meat, ½ Vegetable, ½ Fat

8 ounces uncooked ditalini pasta (small tubes)
6 ounces smoked turkey or chicken breast, skin removed, cut into strips
1 can (15 ounces) light kidney beans, drained and rinsed
½ cup thinly sliced celery
¼ cup chopped red onion
⅓ cup reduced fat mayonnaise
2 tablespoons balsamic vinegar
2 tablespoons chopped fresh chives or green onion
1 tablespoon fresh tarragon *or* 1½ teaspoons dried tarragon leaves
1 teaspoon Dijon mustard
1 clove garlic, minced
¼ teaspoon ground black pepper
   Lettuce leaves (optional)

1 Cook pasta according to package directions, omitting salt. Drain and rinse well under cold water until pasta is cool; drain well.

2 Combine pasta with turkey, beans, celery and onion in medium bowl.

3 Combine mayonnaise, vinegar, chives, tarragon, mustard, garlic and pepper in small bowl. Pour over pasta mixture; toss to coat evenly. Serve on lettuce leaves, if desired.

Makes 7 (1-cup) servings

Cook's Tip

Before adding canned beans to a recipe, drain the beans in a colander and rinse thoroughly with fresh cold water. This will wash away much of the sodium as well as some of the complex sugars that sometimes causes flatulence or stomach gas in some people.

GRILLED RATATOUILLE

The uniqueness of this marinated salad lies in the grilling of the vegetables before serving.

Nutrients per Serving:

Calories	115
(18% of calories from fat)	
Total Fat	2 g
Saturated Fat	<1 g
Cholesterol	0 mg
Sodium	91 mg
Carbohydrate	21 g
Dietary Fiber	3 g
Protein	4 g
Calcium	21 mg
Iron	1 mg
Vitamin A	41 RE
Vitamin C	23 mg

DIETARY EXCHANGES:
1 Starch/Bread, ½ Fat,
1 Vegetable

3 tablespoons red wine vinegar
1 tablespoon olive oil
2 teaspoons fresh thyme
½ teaspoon ground black pepper
4 small Japanese eggplants, cut lengthwise into ½-inch-thick slices
2 small zucchini, cut in half lengthwise
1 medium red onion, quartered
1 red bell pepper, halved and seeded
1 yellow bell pepper, halved and seeded
6 ounces uncooked ziti or penne pasta
½ cup ⅓-less-salt chicken broth
1 tablespoon honey
1 tablespoon Dijon mustard
½ teaspoon Italian seasoning
¼ teaspoon salt
1 cup cherry tomato halves

1 Combine vinegar, oil, thyme and black pepper in shallow bowl. Add eggplants, zucchini, onion and bell peppers; toss to coat evenly. Let stand at room temperature 1 hour or cover and refrigerate overnight.

2 Cook pasta according to package directions, omitting salt. Drain and rinse well under cold water; set aside.

3 Remove vegetables from marinade; reserve marinade. Grill vegetables over medium-hot coals until tender, about 3 to 4 minutes per side. Cool vegetables; cut into 1-inch pieces. Combine vegetables and pasta in large bowl. Add chicken broth, honey, mustard, Italian seasoning and salt to reserved vegetable marinade; whisk to combine. Pour over vegetable-pasta mixture. Gently stir in tomato halves. Serve chilled or at room temperature.

Makes 9 (1-cup) servings

HOT CHINESE CHICKEN SALAD

The "hot" in this recipe stands for temperature and level of spice. If the amount of crushed red pepper is too much for you, simply lower the quantity to satisfy your tastebuds.

Nutrients per Serving:

Calories	164
(30% of calories from fat)	
Total Fat	6 g
Saturated Fat	1 g
Cholesterol	45 mg
Sodium	353 mg
Carbohydrate	12 g
Dietary Fiber	2 g
Protein	17 g
Calcium	34 mg
Iron	2 mg
Vitamin A	81 RE
Vitamin C	55 mg

DIETARY EXCHANGES:
½ Starch/Bread, 2 Lean Meat, 1 Vegetable

8 ounces fresh or steamed Chinese egg noodles
¼ cup ⅓-less-salt chicken broth
2 tablespoons reduced sodium soy sauce
2 tablespoons rice wine vinegar
1 tablespoon rice wine or dry sherry
1 teaspoon sugar
½ teaspoon crushed red pepper
1 tablespoon vegetable oil, divided
1 clove garlic, minced
1½ cups fresh pea pods, sliced diagonally
1 cup thinly sliced green or red bell pepper
1 pound boneless skinless chicken breasts, cut into ½-inch pieces
1 cup thinly sliced red or green cabbage
2 green onions, thinly sliced

1 Cook noodles in boiling water 4 to 5 minutes or until tender. Drain and set aside.

2 Combine chicken broth, soy sauce, vinegar, rice wine, sugar and crushed red pepper in small bowl; set aside.

3 Heat 1 teaspoon oil in large nonstick skillet or wok over high heat. Add garlic, pea pods and bell pepper; cook 1 to 2 minutes or until vegetables are crisp-tender. Set aside.

4 Heat remaining 2 teaspoons oil in skillet. Add chicken and cook 3 to 4 minutes or until chicken is no longer pink. Add cabbage, cooked vegetables and noodles. Stir in sauce; toss to coat evenly. Cook and stir 1 to 2 minutes or until heated through. Sprinkle with green onions before serving. *Makes 6 (1⅓-cup) servings*

GARBANZO PASTA SALAD

Garbanzo beans can be purchased dried or, for simplicity, canned as they are in this recipe. They are known for their high vegetable protein content.

Nutrients per Serving:

Calories	129
(16% of calories from fat)	
Total Fat	2 g
Saturated Fat	<1 g
Cholesterol	1 mg
Sodium	242 mg
Carbohydrate	22 g
Dietary Fiber	3 g
Protein	5 g
Calcium	29 mg
Iron	2 mg
Vitamin A	146 RE
Vitamin C	18 mg

DIETARY EXCHANGES:
1½ Starch/Bread, ½ Fat

4 ounces uncooked spinach rotini or fusilli
1 can (15 ounces) garbanzo beans (chickpeas), drained and rinsed
⅓ cup finely chopped carrot
⅓ cup chopped celery
½ cup chopped red bell pepper
2 green onions with tops, chopped
3 tablespoons balsamic vinegar
2 tablespoons reduced calorie mayonnaise
2 teaspoons prepared whole-grain mustard
½ teaspoon ground black pepper
¼ teaspoon Italian seasoning
　Leaf lettuce

1 Cook pasta according to package directions, omitting salt. Drain and rinse well under cold water until pasta is cool; drain well.

2 Combine pasta, garbanzo beans, carrot, celery, bell pepper and green onions in medium bowl.

3 Whisk together vinegar, mayonnaise, mustard, black pepper and Italian seasoning in small bowl until blended. Pour over salad; toss to coat evenly. Cover and refrigerate up to 8 hours.

4 Arrange lettuce on individual plates. Spoon salad over lettuce and garnish with cherry tomatoes, if desired.　　　　　*Makes 8 (½-cup) servings*

Health Hint
This recipe makes a wonderful vegetarian main-dish salad. To make optimum use of the vegetable protein in the garbanzo beans, serve this salad with a dairy product.

SOUPS

VEGETABLE-CHICKEN NOODLE SOUP

If chicken soup is famous for making you feel better, then this soup should keep you feeling great! Loaded with vegetables, this noodle soup is a wonderful start to any meal.

6 cups ⅓-less-salt chicken broth, divided
1 cup chopped celery
½ cup thinly sliced leek (white part only)
½ cup chopped carrot
½ cup peeled and chopped turnip
1 tablespoon minced fresh parsley
1½ teaspoons fresh thyme *or* ½ teaspoon dried thyme leaves
1 teaspoon fresh rosemary *or* ¼ teaspoon dried rosemary
1 teaspoon balsamic vinegar
¼ teaspoon fresh ground black pepper
2 ounces uncooked "no-yolk" broad noodles
1 cup diced cooked chicken

1 Place ⅓ cup chicken broth, celery, leek, carrot and turnip in large saucepan. Cover and cook over medium heat until vegetables are tender, stirring occasionally.

2 Stir in remaining 5⅔ cups chicken broth, parsley, thyme, rosemary, vinegar and black pepper. Bring to a boil; add noodles. Cook until noodles are tender; stir in chicken. Reduce heat to medium. Simmer until heated through.

Makes 6 (1½-cup) servings

Nutrients per Serving:

Calories	98
(14% of calories from fat)	
Total Fat	2 g
Saturated Fat	<1 g
Cholesterol	18 mg
Sodium	73 mg
Carbohydrate	12 g
Dietary Fiber	1 g
Protein	10 g
Calcium	38 mg
Iron	1 mg
Vitamin A	267 RE
Vitamin C	7 mg

DIETARY EXCHANGES:
½ Starch/Bread, 1 Lean Meat, ½ Vegetable

GREEN CHILE SOUP WITH SPICY BAKED WONTONS

One of the wonders that Christopher Columbus brought from the new world was the mild chili pepper. This enticing recipe comes from the influence of the Szechuan region of China.

Nutrients per Serving:

Calories	150
(24% of calories from fat)	
Total Fat	4 g
Saturated Fat	1 g
Cholesterol	5 mg
Sodium	605 mg
Carbohydrate	32 g
Dietary Fiber	2 g
Protein	5 g
Calcium	199 mg
Iron	2 mg
Vitamin A	159 RE
Vitamin C	44 mg

DIETARY EXCHANGES:
1½ Starch/Bread, ½ Milk, 1 Vegetable, ½ Fat

½ teaspoon chili powder
⅛ teaspoon garlic powder
⅛ teaspoon onion powder
1 teaspoon water
1 teaspoon vegetable oil
12 fresh or frozen, thawed wonton skins
1 tablespoon reduced calorie margarine
1 leek (white part only) thinly sliced
1 cup chopped celery
2 cloves garlic, minced
½ can (7 ounces) ⅓-less-salt chicken broth
1 cup water
2 cans (4 ounces each) chopped green chilies, drained and rinsed
2 cups skim milk
3 tablespoons all-purpose flour
½ teaspoon ground cumin

1 Preheat oven to 375°F. In small bowl, combine chili powder, garlic powder and onion powder. Stir in 1 teaspoon water and oil.

2 Cut wonton skins in half diagonally and place on large ungreased baking sheet. Brush wontons with chili powder mixture. Bake 5 to 6 minutes or until crisp. Cool completely on wire rack.

3 Heat margarine in medium saucepan over medium-high heat. Add leek, celery and garlic; cook 4 minutes or until softened, stirring occasionally. Stir in chicken broth, 1 cup water and chilies. Heat to a boil.

4 Whisk together milk, flour and cumin until smooth. Add milk mixture to saucepan and cook until thickened, stirring constantly, about 4 minutes.

5 Ladle into individual soup bowls. Serve with wontons. Garnish with fresh cilantro, if desired.

Makes 4 (1-cup) servings

JAPANESE NOODLE SOUP

The Japanese udon noodles, called for in this mouth-watering dish, are long, thick wheat noodles with square edges. They are available both fresh and dried.

1 package (8½ ounces) Japanese udon noodles
1 teaspoon vegetable oil
1 medium red bell pepper, cut into thin strips
1 medium carrot, diagonally sliced
2 green onions, thinly sliced
2 cans (14½ ounces each) ⅓-less-salt beef broth
1 cup water
1 teaspoon reduced sodium soy sauce
½ teaspoon grated fresh ginger
½ teaspoon ground black pepper
2 cups thinly sliced fresh shiitake mushrooms, stems removed
4 ounces daikon (Japanese radish), peeled and cut into thin strips
4 ounces firm tofu, drained and cut into ½-inch cubes

1 Cook noodles according to package directions, omitting salt. Drain and rinse; set aside.

2 Heat oil in large nonstick saucepan over medium-high heat. Add red bell pepper, carrot and green onions; cook until slightly softened, about 3 minutes. Stir in beef broth, water, soy sauce, ginger and black pepper. Bring to a boil. Add mushrooms, daikon and tofu. Reduce heat and simmer gently 5 minutes or until heated through.

3 Place noodles in soup tureen or individual bowls. Ladle soup over noodles. Serve immediately.   *Makes 6 (1½-cup) servings*

Nutrients per Serving:

Calories	144
(16% of calories from fat)	
Total Fat	3 g
Saturated Fat	<1 g
Cholesterol	0 mg
Sodium	107 mg
Carbohydrate	24 g
Dietary Fiber	3 g
Protein	9 g
Calcium	56 mg
Iron	3 mg
Vitamin A	374 RE
Vitamin C	16 mg

DIETARY EXCHANGES:
1½ Starch/Bread, ½ Fat,
½ Vegetable

SPICY LENTIL AND PASTA SOUP

Lentils, a popular meat substitute, have a fair amount of calcium and vitamins A and B, and are a good source of iron and phosphorus.

Nutrients per Serving:

Calories	261
(7% of calories from fat)	
Total Fat	2 g
Saturated Fat	<1 g
Cholesterol	1 mg
Sodium	771 mg
Carbohydrate	49 g
Dietary Fiber	5 g
Protein	15 g
Calcium	65 mg
Iron	6 mg
Vitamin A	475 RE
Vitamin C	27 mg

DIETARY EXCHANGES:
2½ Starch/Bread, ½ Lean Meat, 2 Vegetable

2 medium onions, thinly sliced
½ cup chopped carrot
½ cup chopped celery
½ cup peeled and chopped turnip
1 small jalapeño pepper, finely chopped
2 cans (14½ ounces each) clear vegetable broth
1 can (14½ ounces) no-salt-added stewed tomatoes
2 cups water
8 ounces dried lentils
2 teaspoons chili powder
½ teaspoon dried oregano
3 ounces uncooked whole wheat spaghetti, broken
¼ cup minced fresh cilantro

1 Spray large nonstick saucepan with nonstick cooking spray. Add onions, carrot, celery, turnip and jalapeño. Cook over medium heat 10 minutes or until vegetables are crisp-tender.

2 Add broth, tomatoes, water, lentils, chili powder and oregano. Bring to a boil. Reduce heat; cover and simmer 20 to 30 minutes or until lentils are tender.

3 Add pasta and cook 10 minutes or until tender.

4 Ladle soup into bowls; sprinkle with cilantro.   *Makes 6 (1¼-cup) servings*

Cook's Tip
Two ounces of dried long pasta such as spaghetti, is about the same size as the diameter of a quarter.

GINGER WONTON SOUP

A Chinese specialty similar to Italian ravioli, these bite-size dumplings consist of paper-thin dough filled with pork, ricotta cheese, cilantro and Chinese five-spice powder.

Nutrients per Serving:

Calories	259
(17% of calories from fat)	
Total Fat	5 g
Saturated Fat	1 g
Cholesterol	53 mg
Sodium	261 mg
Carbohydrate	39 g
Dietary Fiber	3 g
Protein	16 g
Calcium	74 mg
Iron	3 mg
Vitamin A	72 RE
Vitamin C	43 mg

DIETARY EXCHANGES:
2½ Starch/Bread, 1 Lean Meat, ½ Vegetable, ½ Fat

 4 ounces lean ground pork
½ cup reduced fat ricotta cheese
½ tablespoon minced fresh cilantro
½ teaspoon ground black pepper
⅛ teaspoon Chinese five-spice powder
20 fresh or frozen, thawed wonton skins
 1 teaspoon vegetable oil
⅓ cup chopped red bell pepper
 1 teaspoon grated fresh ginger
 2 cans (14½ ounces each) ⅓-less-salt chicken broth
 2 teaspoons reduced sodium soy sauce
 4 ounces fresh pea pods
 1 can (8¾ ounces) baby corn, drained and rinsed
 2 green onions, thinly sliced

1 Cook pork in small nonstick skillet over medium-high heat 4 minutes or until no longer pink. Cool slightly; stir in ricotta cheese, cilantro, black pepper and five-spice powder.

2 Place 1 teaspoon filling in center of each wonton skin. Fold top corner of wonton over filling. Lightly brush remaining corners with water. Fold left and right corners over filling. Tightly roll filled end toward remaining corner in jelly-roll fashion. Moisten edges with water to seal. Cover and set aside.

3 Heat oil in large saucepan over medium-high heat. Add bell pepper and ginger; cook 1 minute. Add chicken broth and soy sauce; bring to a boil. Add pea pods, baby corn and wontons. Reduce heat to medium-low and simmer 4 to 5 minutes or until wontons are tender. Sprinkle with green onions.   *Makes 4 (1½-cup) servings*

MEDITERRANEAN FISH SOUP

Each bustling Mediterranean seaport has a traditional seafood soup or stew. Within each city, recipes vary according to the day's catch. This energy-packed soup is just a sample of what is overseas.

4 ounces uncooked pastina or other small pasta
¾ cup chopped onion
2 cloves garlic, minced
1 teaspoon fennel seeds
1 can (14½ ounces) no-salt-added stewed tomatoes
1 can (14½ ounces) ⅓-less-salt chicken broth
1 tablespoon minced fresh parsley
½ teaspoon ground black pepper
¼ teaspoon ground turmeric
8 ounces firm, white-fleshed fish, cut into 1-inch pieces
3 ounces raw small shrimp, peeled and deveined

1 Cook pasta according to package directions, omitting salt. Drain and set aside.

2 Spray large nonstick saucepan with nonstick cooking spray. Add onion, garlic and fennel seeds; cook over medium heat 3 minutes or until onion is soft.

3 Stir in tomatoes, chicken broth, parsley, black pepper and turmeric. Bring to a boil; reduce heat and simmer 10 minutes. Add fish and cook 1 minute. Add shrimp and cook until shrimp just begin to turn opaque.

4 Divide pasta among bowls; ladle soup over pasta. *Makes 4 (1½-cup) servings*

Nutrients per Serving:

Calories	209
(10% of calories from fat)	
Total Fat	2 g
Saturated Fat	<1 g
Cholesterol	59 mg
Sodium	111 mg
Carbohydrate	28 g
Dietary Fiber	3 g
Protein	19 g
Calcium	45 mg
Iron	3 mg
Vitamin A	104 RE
Vitamin C	28 mg

DIETARY EXCHANGES:
1½ Starch/Bread, 1½ Lean Meat, 1½ Vegetable

ENTREES

STRAW AND HAY

Delighting in word pictures, the Italians call a combination of green and white noodles "straw and hay." They coat the noodles with a delicate sauce such as this combination of cheese and peas.

Nutrients per Serving:

Calories	348
(11% of calories from fat)	
Total Fat	4 g
Saturated Fat	2 g
Cholesterol	9 mg
Sodium	592 mg
Carbohydrate	52 g
Dietary Fiber	3 g
Protein	25 g
Calcium	187 mg
Iron	2 mg
Vitamin A	106 RE
Vitamin C	6 mg

DIETARY EXCHANGES:
3 Starch/Bread, 2 Lean Meat, ½ Fat

1 cup skim milk
½ cup nonfat cottage cheese
2 teaspoons cornstarch
¼ teaspoon ground mace
⅛ teaspoon ground black pepper
4 ounces uncooked fettuccine noodles
4 ounces uncooked spinach fettuccine noodles
4 ounces reduced fat deli-style ham, diagonally sliced
2 tablespoons chopped chives
1 cup frozen peas, thawed and drained
¼ cup grated Parmesan cheese
⅛ teaspoon paprika

1 Combine milk, cottage cheese, cornstarch, mace and black pepper in blender or food processor; process until smooth. Set aside.

2 Cook noodles according to package directions, omitting salt. Drain and set aside.

3 Spray large nonstick skillet with nonstick cooking spray. Cook and stir ham and chives over medium heat until ham is lightly browned. Stir in milk mixture and peas; cook until thickened.

4 Combine noodles and milk mixture in large bowl. Add Parmesan cheese. Toss to coat evenly. Sprinkle with paprika; serve immediately.   *Makes 4 (1½-cup) servings*

VEGETABLE LASAGNA

Lasagna is a great choice for entertaining. Your guests may never even guess that this vegetable-laden lasagna is meatless.

Nutrients per Serving:

Calories	273
(21% of calories from fat)	
Total Fat	7 g
Saturated Fat	3 g
Cholesterol	19 mg
Sodium	424 mg
Carbohydrate	37 g
Dietary Fiber	6 g
Protein	21 g
Calcium	409 mg
Iron	4 mg
Vitamin A	918 RE
Vitamin C	75 mg

DIETARY EXCHANGES:
1 Starch/Bread, 2 Lean
Meat, 4 Vegetable

Tomato Sauce (page 44)
8 ounces uncooked lasagna noodles (9 noodles)
2 teaspoons olive oil
⅓ cup finely chopped carrot
2 cloves garlic, minced
2 cups coarsely chopped fresh mushrooms
3 cups coarsely chopped broccoli, including stems
1 package (10 ounces) frozen chopped spinach, thawed and drained
⅛ teaspoon ground nutmeg
1 container (15 ounces) nonfat ricotta cheese
2 tablespoons minced fresh parsley
1 tablespoon minced fresh basil
1 tablespoon minced fresh oregano
2 teaspoons cornstarch
¼ teaspoon ground black pepper
1½ cups (6 ounces) shredded part-skim mozzarella cheese, divided
2 tablespoons grated Parmesan cheese

1 Prepare Tomato Sauce. Set aside. Cook noodles according to package directions, omitting salt. Drain and rinse well under cold water. Place noodles on sheet of aluminum foil.

2 Heat olive oil in large nonstick skillet over medium heat. Add carrot and garlic; cook until garlic is soft, about 3 minutes. Add mushrooms; cook and stir until moisture is evaporated. Reduce heat. Add broccoli; cover and simmer 3 to 5 minutes or until broccoli is crisp-tender. Remove from heat; stir in spinach and nutmeg.

3 Preheat oven to 350°F. Combine ricotta cheese, parsley, basil, oregano, cornstarch and black pepper in small bowl. Stir in 1¼ cups mozzarella cheese.

4 Lightly spray 13×9-inch baking dish with nonstick cooking spray. Spread 2 tablespoons Tomato Sauce in bottom of dish. Arrange 3 noodles in dish. Spread with ½ cheese mixture and ½ vegetable mixture. Pour ⅓ tomato sauce over vegetable layer. Repeat layers, ending with noodles. Pour remaining ⅓ tomato sauce over noodles. Sprinkle with Parmesan cheese and remaining ¼ cup mozzarella. Cover; bake 30 minutes. Uncover; continue baking 10 to 15 minutes or until bubbly and heated through. Let stand 10 minutes.

Makes 10 servings

(continued on page 44)

Vegetable Lasagna, continued

TOMATO SAUCE

    2 cans (16 ounces each) whole, peeled tomatoes, undrained
    2 cans (6 ounces each) no-salt-added tomato paste
    1 medium onion, finely chopped
    ¼ cup red wine
    2 cloves garlic, minced
    1 tablespoon Italian seasoning

 Combine tomatoes, tomato paste, onion, red wine, garlic and Italian seasoning in medium saucepan. Cover. Bring to a boil; reduce heat. Simmer 20 minutes.

Health Hint

Tomatoes are an excellent source of antioxidants. Studies suggest that antioxidants may reduce the risk of some forms of cancer, heart disease, strokes, as well as slow the aging process.

❖

KOREAN-STYLE BEEF AND PASTA

Rice noodles, also known as rice sticks, are made from rice flour and are as thin as string. They are usually coiled into nests and packaged in plastic bags.

Nutrients per Serving:

Calories	194
(19% of calories from fat)	
Total Fat	4 g
Saturated Fat	1 g
Cholesterol	29 mg
Sodium	668 mg
Carbohydrate	24 g
Dietary Fiber	1 g
Protein	13 g
Calcium	37 mg
Iron	3 mg
Vitamin A	309 RE
Vitamin C	37 mg

DIETARY EXCHANGES:
1½ Starch/Bread, 1½ Lean Meat, ½ Vegetable

¾ pound lean round steak
2 tablespoons reduced sodium soy sauce
1 tablespoon rice wine
2 teaspoons sugar
  Korean-Style Dressing (page 46)
1 package (6¾ ounces) rice noodles
2 cups thinly sliced napa cabbage
1¾ cups thinly sliced yellow bell peppers
½ cup thinly sliced radishes
1 medium carrot, shredded
2 green onions, thinly sliced

1 Freeze beef until partially firm; cut into very thin slices.

2 Combine soy sauce, rice wine and sugar in small nonmetallic bowl. Add beef slices; toss to coat evenly. Cover and refrigerate 8 hours or overnight.

3 Drain beef; grill over medium-hot coals 2 to 3 minutes or until desired doneness.

4 Meanwhile, prepare Korean-Style Dressing; set aside.

5 Cook noodles in boiling water 1 to 2 minutes or until tender; drain and rinse under cold water. Arrange noodles on platter.

6 Combine cabbage, bell peppers, radishes, carrot, green onions and beef in medium bowl. Add Korean-Style Dressing; toss to coat evenly. Serve over noodles. Garnish with green onion brush and carrot ribbons, if desired.   *Makes 8 (1-cup) servings*

(continued on page 46)

Korean-Style Beef and Pasta, continued

KOREAN-STYLE DRESSING

   2 teaspoons sesame seeds
   ⅓ cup orange juice
   2 tablespoons rice wine
   2 teaspoons reduced sodium soy sauce
   1 teaspoon Oriental sesame oil
   1 teaspoon grated fresh ginger
   1 teaspoon sugar
   1 clove garlic, minced
   ⅛ teaspoon crushed red pepper

1 Place sesame seeds in small nonstick skillet. Cook and stir over medium heat until lightly browned and toasted, about 5 minutes. Cool completely.

2 Crush sesame seeds using mortar and pestle or with wooden spoon; transfer to small bowl.

3 Add orange juice, rice wine, soy sauce, sesame oil, ginger, sugar, garlic and crushed red pepper to sesame seeds. Blend well.

❖

Cook's Tip

When peeling fresh ginger, be careful to remove only the skin because the flesh just under the surface is the most flavorful part.

❖

CHEESE TORTELLINI WITH TUNA

Cheese tortellini and tuna both provide good sources of protein. Add a green salad to complete this delicious meal.

1 tuna steak* (about 6 ounces)
1 package (9 ounces) reduced fat cheese tortellini
1 cup finely chopped red bell pepper
1 cup finely chopped green bell pepper
¼ cup finely chopped onion
¾ teaspoon fennel seeds, crushed
½ cup evaporated skim milk
2 teaspoons all-purpose flour
½ teaspoon dry mustard
½ teaspoon ground black pepper

1 Grill or broil tuna 4 inches from heat source until fish just begins to flake, about 7 to 9 minutes. Remove and discard skin. Cut tuna into chunks; set aside.

2 Cook pasta according to package directions, omitting salt. Drain; set aside.

3 Spray large nonstick skillet with nonstick cooking spray. Add bell peppers, onion and fennel seeds; cook over medium heat until crisp-tender.

4 Whisk together milk, flour, mustard and black pepper in small bowl until smooth; add to skillet. Cook until thickened, stirring constantly. Stir in tuna and pasta; reduce heat and simmer until heated through, about 3 minutes. Serve immediately.

Makes about 4 (1½-cup) servings

*Or, substitute 1 can (6 ounces) tuna packed in water, drained, for tuna steak.

Nutrients per Serving:

Calories	180
(19% of calories from fat)	
Total Fat	4 g
Saturated Fat	2 g
Cholesterol	21 mg
Sodium	160 mg
Carbohydrate	21 g
Dietary Fiber	3 g
Protein	16 g
Calcium	141 mg
Iron	2 mg
Vitamin A	397 RE
Vitamin C	112 mg

DIETARY EXCHANGES:
½ Starch/Bread, 1½ Lean Meat, ½ Milk, 1 Vegetable

PAD THAI

This lighter version of the traditional Thai dish is an excellent choice when you're in the mood for something just a little different.

❖

Nutrients per Serving:

Calories	265
(18% of calories from fat)	
Total Fat	6 g
Saturated Fat	1 g
Cholesterol	38 mg
Sodium	798 mg
Carbohydrate	42 g
Dietary Fiber	1 g
Protein	14 g
Calcium	78 mg
Iron	2 mg
Vitamin A	453 RE
Vitamin C	13 mg

DIETARY EXCHANGES:
2½ Starch/Bread, ½ Lean
Meat, 1 Vegetable, ½ Fat

8 ounces uncooked rice noodles, ⅛ inch wide
1½ tablespoons fish sauce*
1 to 2 tablespoons fresh lemon juice
2 tablespoons rice wine vinegar
1 tablespoon ketchup
2 teaspoons sugar
¼ teaspoon crushed red pepper
1 tablespoon vegetable oil
4 ounces boneless skinless chicken breast, finely chopped
2 green onions, thinly sliced
2 cloves garlic, minced
3 ounces raw small shrimp, peeled and deveined
2 cups fresh bean sprouts
1 medium carrot, shredded
3 tablespoons minced fresh cilantro
2 tablespoons chopped unsalted dry-roasted peanuts

1 Place noodles in medium bowl. Cover with lukewarm water and let stand 30 minutes or until soft. Drain and set aside. Whisk together fish sauce, lemon juice, rice wine vinegar, ketchup, sugar and crushed red pepper in small bowl; set aside.

2 Heat oil in wok or large nonstick skillet over medium-high heat. Add chicken, green onions and garlic. Cook and stir until chicken is no longer pink. Stir in noodles; cook 1 minute. Add shrimp and bean sprouts; cook just until shrimp turn opaque, about 3 minutes. Stir in fish sauce mixture; toss to coat evenly. Cook until heated through, about 2 minutes.

3 Arrange noodle mixture on platter; sprinkle with carrot, cilantro and peanuts. Garnish with lemon wedges, tomato wedges and fresh cilantro, if desired.

Makes 5 (1-cup) servings

*Fish sauce is available at most larger supermarkets and Oriental markets.

SWEET POTATO RAVIOLI WITH ASIAGO CHEESE SAUCE

One culinary idea that knows no boundaries is stuffed pasta pillows, otherwise called ravioli. This gourmet entrée takes a step past the ordinary by combining the flavors of sweet potato, yogurt, sage and Asiago cheese. The result is outstanding!

Nutrients per Serving:

Calories	304
(20% of calories from fat)	
Total Fat	7 g
Saturated Fat	3 g
Cholesterol	19 mg
Sodium	558 mg
Carbohydrate	49 g
Dietary Fiber	3 g
Protein	11 g
Calcium	174 mg
Iron	2 mg
Vitamin A	1530 RE
Vitamin C	17 mg

DIETARY EXCHANGES:
3 Starch/Bread, ½ Lean
Meat, 1 Fat

¾ pound sweet potatoes
2 tablespoons plain nonfat yogurt
1 tablespoon plus ¼ teaspoon minced fresh sage, divided
1 teaspoon minced fresh chives
24 wonton wrappers
1 tablespoon reduced calorie margarine
1 tablespoon plus 2 teaspoons all-purpose flour
½ cup skim milk
½ cup ⅓-less-salt chicken broth
½ cup (2 ounces) shredded Asiago or Cheddar cheese
¼ teaspoon ground nutmeg
¼ teaspoon ground white pepper
⅛ teaspoon ground cinnamon

1 Preheat oven to 350°F. Bake sweet potatoes 40 to 45 minutes or until tender. Cool completely. Peel potatoes and mash pulp in small bowl. Stir in yogurt, ¼ teaspoon sage and chives.

2 Place wonton wrappers on counter. Spoon 1 rounded teaspoon potato mixture in center of each wonton. Spread filling flat leaving ½-inch border. Brush edges lightly with water. Fold wontons in half diagonally, pressing lightly to seal. Place filled wontons on baking sheet and cover loosely with plastic wrap.

3 Bring 1½ quarts water to a boil in large saucepan. Reduce heat to medium. Add a few ravioli at a time. (Do not overcrowd.) Cook until tender, about 9 minutes. Transfer to platter with slotted spoon.

4 Melt margarine in small saucepan over medium heat. Stir in flour; cook 1 minute, stirring constantly. Gradually stir in milk and chicken broth. Cook and stir until slightly thickened, about 4 minutes. Stir in cheese, nutmeg, white pepper and cinnamon.

5 Spoon 3 tablespoons sauce onto individual plates. Place 3 ravioli onto each plate. Sprinkle with remaining sage.   *Makes 8 servings*

EASY TEX-MEX BAKE

Tex-Mex is quickly becoming one of the most requested flavor combinations. If that is the taste you're looking for, you won't be disappointed with this low fat dish.

8 ounces uncooked thin mostaccioli
1 pound ground turkey breast
1 package (10 ounces) frozen corn, thawed, drained
⅔ cup bottled medium or mild salsa
1 container (16 ounces) low fat cottage cheese
1 egg
1 tablespoon minced fresh cilantro
½ teaspoon ground white pepper
¼ teaspoon ground cumin
½ cup (2 ounces) shredded Monterey Jack cheese

1 Cook pasta according to package directions, omitting salt. Drain and rinse well; set aside.

2 Spray large nonstick skillet with nonstick cooking spray. Add turkey; cook over high heat until no longer pink, about 5 minutes. Stir in corn and salsa. Remove from heat.

3 Preheat oven to 350°F. Combine cottage cheese, egg, cilantro, white pepper and cumin in small bowl.

4 Spoon ½ turkey mixture in bottom of 11½×7½-inch baking dish. Top with pasta. Spoon cottage cheese mixture over pasta. Top with remaining turkey mixture. Sprinkle Monterey Jack cheese over casserole.

5 Bake 25 to 30 minutes or until heated through. *Makes 6 servings*

Nutrients per Serving:

Calories	365
(15% of calories from fat)	
Total Fat	6 g
Saturated Fat	3 g
Cholesterol	99 mg
Sodium	800 mg
Carbohydrate	39 g
Dietary Fiber	4 g
Protein	38 g
Calcium	147 mg
Iron	3 mg
Vitamin A	166 RE
Vitamin C	26 mg

DIETARY EXCHANGES:
2 Starch/Bread, 4 Lean Meat

PASTA PRIMAVERA

In Italian, primavera means "spring style." By including so many fresh vegetables, this famous entrée has been referred to as a "garden on a plate."

8 ounces uncooked linguine or medium pasta shells
1 tablespoon reduced calorie margarine
2 green onions, diagonally sliced
1 clove garlic, minced
1 cup fresh mushroom slices
1 cup broccoli florets
2½ cups fresh snow peas
4 to 8 asparagus spears, cut into 2-inch pieces
1 medium red bell pepper, cut into thin strips
½ cup evaporated skimmed milk
½ teaspoon dried tarragon leaves
½ teaspoon ground black pepper
⅓ cup grated Parmesan cheese

1 Cook pasta according to package directions, omitting salt. Drain and set aside.

2 Melt margarine in large nonstick skillet over medium-high heat. Add green onions and garlic; cook until softened. Add mushrooms and broccoli. Cover. Cook 3 minutes or until mushrooms are tender.

3 Add snow peas, asparagus, bell pepper, milk, tarragon and black pepper. Cook and stir until vegetables are crisp-tender and lightly coated.

4 Add cheese; toss to coat evenly. Serve immediately.   *Makes 4 (2-cup) servings*

Nutrients per Serving:

Calories	329
(16% of calories from fat)	
Total Fat	6 g
Saturated Fat	2 g
Cholesterol	8 mg
Sodium	243 mg
Carbohydrate	51 g
Dietary Fiber	6 g
Protein	18 g
Calcium	265 mg
Iron	4 mg
Vitamin A	167 RE
Vitamin C	82 mg

DIETARY EXCHANGES:
2½ Starch/Bread, ½ Lean Meat, 1½ Vegetable, ½ Milk

FAJITA STUFFED SHELLS

*Mexican and Italian meet in
this enticing entrée.
Flavored with lime, garlic,
oregano, cumin and
cilantro, it tastes much more
complicated than it is.*

¼ cup fresh lime juice
1 clove garlic, minced
½ teaspoon dried oregano leaves
¼ teaspoon ground cumin
1 (6-ounce) boneless lean round or flank steak
1 medium green bell pepper, halved and seeded
1 medium onion, cut in half
12 uncooked jumbo pasta shells (about 6 ounces)
½ cup reduced fat sour cream
2 tablespoons shredded reduced fat Cheddar cheese
1 tablespoon minced fresh cilantro
⅔ cup bottled chunky salsa
2 cups shredded leaf lettuce

1 Combine lime juice, garlic, oregano and cumin in shallow nonmetallic dish. Add steak, bell pepper and onion. Cover and refrigerate 8 hours or overnight.

2 Preheat oven to 350°F. Cook pasta shells according to package directions, omitting salt. Drain and rinse well under cold water; set aside.

3 Grill steak and vegetables over medium-hot coals 3 to 4 minutes per side or until desired doneness; cool slightly. Cut steak into thin slices. Chop vegetables. Place steak slices and vegetables in medium bowl. Stir in sour cream, Cheddar cheese and cilantro. Stuff shells evenly with meat mixture, mounding slightly.

4 Arrange shells in 8-inch baking dish. Pour salsa over filled shells. Cover with foil and bake 15 minutes or until heated through. Divide lettuce evenly among 4 plates; arrange 3 shells on each plate. *Makes 4 servings*

Nutrients per Serving:	
Calories	265
(16% of calories from fat)	
Total Fat	5 g
Saturated Fat	2 g
Cholesterol	33 mg
Sodium	341 mg
Carbohydrate	36 g
Dietary Fiber	3 g
Protein	19 g
Calcium	98 mg
Iron	3 mg
Vitamin A	99 RE
Vitamin C	38 mg

DIETARY EXCHANGES:
2 Starch/Bread, 1½ Lean
Meat, 1 Vegetable

JAMBALAYA

In Italian, orzo means "barley," but it is actually a tiny, rice-shaped pasta. It is ideal for soups and wonderful when served as a substitute for rice, as it is in this spicy dish.

Nutrients per Serving:

Calories	359
(11% of calories from fat)	
Total Fat	5 g
Saturated Fat	1 g
Cholesterol	24 mg
Sodium	728 mg
Carbohydrate	62 g
Dietary Fiber	11 g
Protein	20 g
Calcium	113 mg
Iron	5 mg
Vitamin A	156 RE
Vitamin C	102 mg

DIETARY EXCHANGES:
3 Starch/Bread, 1 Lean
Meat, 3 Vegetable

2 teaspoons vegetable oil
4 ounces smoked chicken, cubed
1½ cups chopped green bell pepper
1¼ cups chopped celery
1 cup chopped onion
3 cloves garlic, minced
1 can (16 ounces) no-salt-added tomatoes, undrained and cut up
2 bay leaves
½ teaspoon dried thyme leaves
¼ teaspoon dry mustard
¼ teaspoon ground black pepper
3 to 5 dashes hot pepper sauce
1 cup uncooked orzo pasta
1 can (15.5 ounces) red kidney beans, drained and rinsed
¼ cup thinly sliced green onions

1 Heat oil in large nonstick saucepan over medium-high heat. Add chicken and cook until lightly browned, about 2 minutes. Add bell pepper, celery, onion and garlic. Cook, stirring frequently, 5 minutes or until vegetables are tender.

2 Add tomatoes, bay leaves, thyme, mustard, black pepper and hot pepper sauce. Bring to a boil; reduce heat and simmer 10 minutes or until slightly thickened. Remove bay leaves.

3 Cook pasta according to package directions, omitting salt. Drain, but do not rinse.

4 Stir beans into tomato mixture. Cook 5 minutes or until heated through.

5 Spoon approximately ½ cup pasta into individual bowls. Spoon jambalaya over pasta. Sprinkle with green onions. Garnish as desired. *Makes 4 servings*

CHICKEN CHOW MEIN

Chow Mein is a Chinese-American dish consisting of bits of meat and vegetables traditionally served over crispy fried noodles. This lighter version eliminates the extra fat and calories by baking the noodles instead.

Nutrients per Serving:

Calories	284
(6% of calories from fat)	
Total Fat	2 g
Saturated Fat	<1 g
Cholesterol	22 mg
Sodium	322 mg
Carbohydrate	52 g
Dietary Fiber	3 g
Protein	16 g
Calcium	57 mg
Iron	3 mg
Vitamin A	350 RE
Vitamin C	23 mg

DIETARY EXCHANGES:
2 Starch/Bread, 1 Lean Meat, 3 Vegetable

6 ounces uncooked fresh Chinese egg noodles
  Nonstick cooking spray
½ cup ⅓-less-salt chicken broth
2 tablespoons reduced sodium soy sauce
1½ teaspoons cornstarch
½ teaspoon Oriental sesame oil
½ teaspoon ground black pepper
⅛ teaspoon Chinese five-spice powder
6 ounces boneless skinless chicken breasts, coarsely chopped
2 green onions, sliced
2 cups thinly sliced bok choy
1½ cups mixed frozen vegetables, thawed and drained
1 can (8 ounces) sliced water chestnuts, drained and rinsed
1 cup fresh bean sprouts

1 Preheat oven to 400°F. Cook noodles according to package directions, omitting salt. Drain and rinse well under cold water until pasta is cool; drain well. Lightly spray 9-inch cake pan with nonstick cooking spray. Spread noodles in pan, pressing firmly. Lightly spray top of noodles with nonstick cooking spray. Bake 10 minutes.

2 Invert noodles onto baking sheet or large plate. Carefully slide noodle cake back into cake pan. Bake 10 to 15 minutes or until top is crisp and lightly browned. Transfer to serving platter. Whisk together chicken broth, soy sauce, cornstarch, sesame oil, black pepper and five-spice powder in small bowl until cornstarch is dissolved; set aside.

3 Spray large nonstick skillet with nonstick cooking spray. Add chicken and green onions. Cook over medium-high heat, stirring frequently, until chicken is no longer pink, about 5 minutes. Stir in bok choy, mixed vegetables and water chestnuts. Cook 3 minutes or until vegetables are crisp-tender. Push vegetables to one side of skillet; stir in sauce. Cook and stir until thickened, about 2 minutes. Stir in bean sprouts. Spoon over noodle cake.

Makes 4 servings

DOUBLE SPINACH BAKE

Cooked spinach explodes with vitamin A and beta-carotene! This entrée packs a double punch by using spinach fettuccine.

Nutrients per Serving:

Calories	235
(9% of calories from fat)	
Total Fat	3 g
Saturated Fat	<1 g
Cholesterol	46 mg
Sodium	110 mg
Carbohydrate	41 g
Dietary Fiber	1 g
Protein	19 g
Calcium	57 mg
Iron	1 mg
Vitamin A	280 RE
Vitamin C	12 mg

DIETARY EXCHANGES:
2 Starch/Bread, 1½ Lean Meat, ½ Vegetable

8 ounces uncooked spinach fettuccine noodles
1 cup fresh mushroom slices
1 green onion with top, finely chopped
1 clove garlic, minced
4 to 5 cups fresh spinach, coarsely chopped *or* 1 package (10 ounces) frozen spinach, thawed and drained
1 tablespoon water
1 container (15 ounces) nonfat ricotta cheese
¼ cup skim milk
1 egg
½ teaspoon ground nutmeg
½ teaspoon ground black pepper
¼ cup (1 ounce) shredded reduced fat Swiss cheese

1 Preheat oven to 350°F. Cook pasta according to package directions, omitting salt. Drain; set aside.

2 Spray medium skillet with nonstick cooking spray. Add mushrooms, green onion and garlic. Cook and stir over medium heat until mushrooms are softened. Add spinach and water. Cover; cook until spinach is wilted, about 3 minutes.

3 Combine ricotta cheese, milk, egg, nutmeg and black pepper in large bowl. Gently stir in noodles and vegetables; toss to coat evenly.

4 Lightly coat shallow 1½-quart casserole with nonstick cooking spray. Spread noodle mixture in casserole. Sprinkle with Swiss cheese.

5 Bake 25 to 30 minutes or until knife inserted halfway to center comes out clean.

Makes 6 (1-cup) servings

ENLIGHTENED MACARONI AND CHEESE

This twist on an all-time American favorite is guaranteed to make your family smile, and it's low in fat too!

Nutrients per Serving:

Calories	266
(19% of calories from fat)	
Total Fat	6 g
Saturated Fat	3 g
Cholesterol	18 mg
Sodium	200 mg
Carbohydrate	35 g
Dietary Fiber	2 g
Protein	18 g
Calcium	406 mg
Iron	2 mg
Vitamin A	125 RE
Vitamin C	11 mg

DIETARY EXCHANGES:
2 Starch/Bread, 1 Lean
Meat, ½ Milk, ½ Fat

8 ounces uncooked wagon wheel, bow tie or elbow pasta
1 tablespoon all-purpose flour
2 teaspoons cornstarch
¼ teaspoon dry mustard
1 can (12 ounces) evaporated skimmed milk
1 cup (4 ounces) shredded reduced fat medium sharp Cheddar cheese
½ cup (2 ounces) shredded reduced fat Monterey Jack cheese
1 jar (2 ounces) diced pimiento, drained and rinsed
1 teaspoon Worcestershire sauce
¼ teaspoon ground black pepper
1 tablespoon dry bread crumbs
1 tablespoon paprika

1 Preheat oven to 375°F.

2 Cook pasta according to package directions, omitting salt. Drain and set aside.

3 Combine flour, cornstarch and mustard in medium saucepan; stir in milk until smooth. Cook over low heat, stirring occasionally, until slightly thickened, about 8 minutes.

4 Remove from heat; stir in cheeses, pimiento, Worcestershire sauce and black pepper. Add pasta; mix well.

5 Spray 1½-quart casserole with nonstick cooking spray. Spoon mixture into casserole; sprinkle with bread crumbs and paprika.

6 Bake 20 minutes or until bubbly and heated through.   *Makes 6 (1-cup) servings*

CHICKEN NOODLE ROLL-UPS

Serve this colorful lasagna-like dish for a special occasion!

Nutrients per Serving:

Calories	179
(22% of calories from fat)	
Total Fat	4 g
Saturated Fat	1 g
Cholesterol	46 mg
Sodium	291 mg
Carbohydrate	17 g
Dietary Fiber	2 g
Protein	18 g
Calcium	77 mg
Iron	1 mg
Vitamin A	95 RE
Vitamin C	24 mg

DIETARY EXCHANGES:
1 Starch/Bread, 2 Lean Meat

9 uncooked lasagna noodles (about 9 ounces)
8 ounces boneless skinless chicken breasts, cut into chunks
2 cups finely chopped broccoli
2 cups low fat cottage cheese
1 egg
2 teaspoons minced fresh chives
¼ teaspoon ground nutmeg
¼ teaspoon ground black pepper
1 tablespoon reduced calorie margarine
2 tablespoons all-purpose flour
1 cup ⅓-less-salt chicken broth
½ cup skim milk
½ teaspoon dry mustard
1 medium tomato, seeded and chopped

1 Cook lasagna noodles according to package directions, omitting salt. Drain and rinse well under cold water. Place in single layer on aluminum foil.

2 Preheat oven to 375°F. Place chicken in food processor or blender; process until finely chopped. Spray large nonstick skillet with nonstick cooking spray; place over medium heat. Add chicken; cook 4 minutes or until chicken is no longer pink. Stir in broccoli; cook until broccoli is crisp-tender, about 3 minutes. Cool.

3 Combine cottage cheese, egg, chives, nutmeg and black pepper in medium bowl. Stir in chicken mixture. Spread generous ⅓ cup filling over each lasagna noodle. Roll up noodles, starting at short end. Place filled rolls, seam side down, in 10×8-inch baking dish; set aside.

4 Melt margarine in small saucepan over medium-high heat. Stir in flour; cook 1 minute. Whisk in chicken broth, milk and mustard. Cook, stirring constantly, until thickened. Pour sauce over filled rolls; sprinkle with tomato. Cover dish with foil. Bake 30 to 35 minutes or until filling is set.

Makes 9 servings

ORANGE BEEF AND BROCCOLI

Broccoli is said to be one of the healthiest foods you can eat! It is loaded with antioxidants and cancer-fighting agents, such as vitamin C.

1 pound lean boneless sirloin, cut 1 inch thick
½ cup orange juice
2 teaspoons reduced sodium soy sauce
1 teaspoon sugar
3 teaspoons vegetable oil, divided
¾ pound broccoli, coarsely chopped
1 cup diagonally sliced carrots
½ cup thinly sliced red bell pepper
1 green onion, diagonally sliced
2 teaspoons cornstarch
¾ cup cold water
1 tablespoon grated orange peel
6 ounces uncooked "no-yolk" broad noodles

1 Slice beef across grain into ⅛-inch-thick slices. Place beef strips in medium glass or nonmetallic bowl. Add orange juice, soy sauce and sugar; toss to coat evenly. Let stand 30 minutes, or cover and refrigerate overnight.

2 Heat 2 teaspoons oil in large nonstick skillet or wok over high heat. Add broccoli, carrots, bell pepper and green onion. Cook 2 minutes, stirring frequently. Remove vegetables to large bowl.

3 Heat remaining 1 teaspoon oil in skillet. Drain beef strips; reserve marinade. Add beef to skillet; cook 1 to 2 minutes or until no longer pink. Add vegetables and reserved marinade to skillet. Bring to a boil. Stir cornstarch into water until smooth. Add to skillet and cook until thickened, stirring constantly. Sprinkle with grated orange peel.

4 Cook noodles according to package directions, omitting salt. Drain. Spoon beef mixture over noodles and serve immediately. Garnish with orange curls, if desired.

Makes 4 servings

Nutrients per Serving:

Calories	424
(27% of calories from fat)	
Total Fat	13 g
Saturated Fat	3 g
Cholesterol	77 mg
Sodium	169 mg
Carbohydrate	43 g
Dietary Fiber	6 g
Protein	35 g
Calcium	69 mg
Iron	5 mg
Vitamin A	943 RE
Vitamin C	125 mg

DIETARY EXCHANGES:
2 Starch/Bread, 3½ Lean Meat, 2½ Vegetable, ½ Fat

SANTA FE FUSILLI

When you have a taste for something hearty and healthy, this full-flavored Texas-style dish is for you!

Nutrients per Serving:

Calories	228
(9% of calories from fat)	
Total Fat	2 g
Saturated Fat	<1 g
Cholesterol	3 mg
Sodium	215 mg
Carbohydrate	46 g
Dietary Fiber	8 g
Protein	12 g
Calcium	41 mg
Iron	2 mg
Vitamin A	189 RE
Vitamin C	57 mg

DIETARY EXCHANGES:
2 Starch/Bread, ½ Lean
Meat, 2½ Vegetable

1 medium red bell pepper*
2 teaspoons cumin seeds
¾ cup chopped, seeded tomato
¼ cup chopped onion
1 clove garlic, minced
1 tablespoon chili powder
¼ teaspoon crushed red pepper
¼ teaspoon ground black pepper
1 can (16 ounces) no-salt-added tomato purée
⅓ cup water
1 teaspoon sugar
8 ounces uncooked fusilli pasta
1 can (16 ounces) black beans, drained and rinsed
1 package (10 ounces) frozen corn, thawed and drained
1 can (4 ounces) chopped green chilies, drained
⅓ cup low fat sour cream
Fresh cilantro

1 Roast bell pepper over charcoal or gas flame or place under broiler, turning several times, until skin is charred. Cool 10 minutes. Peel and discard charred skin. Cut pepper in half; seed and coarsely chop.

2 Place cumin seeds in large nonstick saucepan. Cook and stir over medium heat until lightly toasted, about 3 minutes. Stir in tomato, onion, garlic, chili powder, crushed red pepper and black pepper. Cook until vegetables are tender, about 5 minutes. Stir in tomato purée, water and sugar. Reduce heat to low. Cover and simmer 15 minutes.

3 Cook pasta according to package directions, omitting salt. Drain and set aside. Stir in beans, corn and chilies into vegetable mixture. Cook until heated through, about 8 minutes. Stir in pasta. Spoon into individual bowls; top with sour cream and cilantro.

Makes 8 (1-cup) servings

*Or, substitute 1 jar (7 ounces) roasted peppers, drained and chopped and omit step 1.

PLUM CHICKEN

❖

Plums are one of the world's most popular fruits. Choose plums that are firm but not hard. Look for plumpness and full color. Avoid plums with breaks in the skin and brownish discoloration.

❖

Nutrients per Serving:

Calories	415
(11% of calories from fat)	
Total Fat	5 g
Saturated Fat	1 g
Cholesterol	43 mg
Sodium	307 mg
Carbohydrate	73 g
Dietary Fiber	3 g
Protein	21 g
Calcium	49 mg
Iron	3 mg
Vitamin A	33 RE
Vitamin C	30 mg

DIETARY EXCHANGES:
3 Starch/Bread, 1½ Lean
Meat, 1 Vegetable,
1½ Fruit

6 ounces fresh uncooked Chinese egg noodles
¼ cup plum preserves or jam
3 tablespoons rice wine vinegar
3 tablespoons reduced sodium soy sauce
1 tablespoon cornstarch
3 teaspoons oil, divided
1 small red onion, thinly sliced
2 cups fresh pea pods, diagonally sliced
12 ounces boneless skinless chicken breasts, cut into thin strips
4 medium plums or apricots, pitted and sliced

1 Cook noodles according to package directions, omitting salt. Drain and keep warm.

2 Stir together plum preserves, rice wine vinegar, soy sauce and cornstarch; set aside.

3 Heat 2 teaspoons oil in large nonstick skillet or wok over high heat. Add onion and cook 2 minutes or until slightly softened. Add pea pods and cook 3 minutes. Remove vegetables to medium bowl.

4 Heat remaining 1 teaspoon oil in skillet. Add chicken and cook over medium-high heat 2 to 3 minutes or until no longer pink. Push chicken to one side of skillet.

5 Stir sauce; add to skillet. Cook and stir until thick and bubbly. Stir in vegetables and plums; coat evenly. Cook 3 minutes or until heated through. Toss with noodles and serve immediately.

Makes 4 servings

PASTITSO

Replacing real eggs with egg substitute in this fabulous Greek dish significantly reduces the amount of cholesterol normally found here.

Nutrients per Serving:

Calories	280
(15% of calories from fat)	
Total Fat	5 g
Saturated Fat	2 g
Cholesterol	31 mg
Sodium	366 mg
Carbohydrate	39 g
Dietary Fiber	1 g
Protein	20 g
Calcium	134 mg
Iron	3 mg
Vitamin A	198 RE
Vitamin C	4 mg

DIETARY EXCHANGES:
2½ Starch/Bread, 1½ Lean Meat, ½ Vegetable

8 ounces uncooked elbow macaroni
½ cup cholesterol free egg substitute
¼ teaspoon ground nutmeg
¾ pound lean ground lamb, beef or turkey
½ cup chopped onion
1 clove garlic, minced
1 can (8 ounces) tomato sauce
¾ teaspoon dried mint leaves
½ teaspoon dried oregano leaves
½ teaspoon ground black pepper
⅛ teaspoon ground cinnamon
2 teaspoons reduced calorie margarine
3 tablespoons all-purpose flour
1½ cups skim milk
2 tablespoons grated Parmesan cheese

1 Cook pasta according to package directions, omitting salt. Drain and transfer to medium bowl; stir in egg substitute and nutmeg.

2 Lightly spray bottom of 9-inch square baking dish with nonstick cooking spray. Spread pasta mixture in bottom of baking dish. Set aside.

3 Preheat oven to 350°F. Cook lamb, onion and garlic in large nonstick skillet over medium heat until lamb is no longer pink. Stir in tomato sauce, mint, oregano, black pepper and cinnamon. Reduce heat and simmer 10 minutes; spread over pasta.

4 Melt margarine in small nonstick saucepan over medium-high heat. Add flour. Stir constantly for 1 minute. Whisk in milk. Cook, stirring constantly, until thickened, about 6 minutes; spread over meat mixture. Sprinkle with Parmesan cheese. Bake 30 to 40 minutes or until set.

Makes 6 servings

THAI BEEF NOODLES

Today more than ever, lean beef can be included in heart-healthy diets. This fabulous dish incorporates many traditional Thai ingredients—without all the fat.

1 pound lean boneless top sirloin, cut 1 inch thick
2 tablespoons reduced sodium soy sauce, divided
2 tablespoons rice wine or dry sherry
2 teaspoons sugar
2 tablespoons water
1 tablespoon creamy peanut butter
2 teaspoons rice wine vinegar
¼ teaspoon crushed red pepper
⅛ teaspoon grated fresh ginger
6 ounces uncooked vermicelli or other pasta
1 cup chopped red bell pepper
¾ cup chopped, seeded cucumber
¼ cup diagonally sliced green onions

1 Cut steak into 1-inch pieces; place in medium glass or nonmetallic bowl. Add 1 tablespoon soy sauce, rice wine and sugar to beef; toss to coat evenly. Let stand 30 minutes, or cover and refrigerate overnight.

2 Combine remaining 1 tablespoon soy sauce, water, peanut butter, rice wine vinegar, crushed red pepper and ginger in large bowl.

3 Cook pasta according to package directions, omitting salt. Drain and rinse well under hot water. Add pasta to peanut butter mixture; toss to coat evenly. Set aside. Drain beef; discard marinade.

4 Spray large nonstick skillet with nonstick cooking spray; heat over medium-high heat. Add beef and bell pepper to skillet. Cook 2 to 3 minutes or until desired doneness. Add beef and bell pepper to pasta mixture; toss to coat evenly. Sprinkle with cucumber and green onions.

Makes 4 servings

Nutrients per Serving:

Calories	400
(29% of calories from fat)	
Total Fat	13 g
Saturated Fat	4 g
Cholesterol	76 mg
Sodium	790 mg
Carbohydrate	40 g
Dietary Fiber	1 g
Protein	33 g
Calcium	35 mg
Iron	5 mg
Vitamin A	48 RE
Vitamin C	52 mg

DIETARY EXCHANGES:
2½ Starch/Bread, 3½ Lean Meat, 1 Vegetable, ½ Fat

SIDE DISHES

LEMON TOSSED LINGUINE

Lemon is rapidly becoming an appealing substitute for high fat sauces. Once you've tried this exceptional combination, you may never go back to your original sauces.

8 ounces uncooked linguine noodles
3 tablespoons fresh lemon juice
2 teaspoons reduced calorie margarine
2 tablespoons minced chives
⅓ cup skim milk
1 teaspoon cornstarch
1 tablespoon minced fresh dill *or* 1 teaspoon dried dill weed
1 tablespoon minced fresh parsley *or* 1 teaspoon dried parsley
2 teaspoons grated lemon peel
¼ teaspoon ground white pepper
3 tablespoons grated Romano or Parmesan cheese

1 Cook noodles according to package directions, omitting salt. Drain well. Place in medium bowl; pour lemon juice over noodles.

2 Meanwhile, melt margarine in small saucepan over medium heat. Add chives and cook until chives are soft. Combine milk and cornstarch; stir into saucepan. Cook and stir until thickened. Stir in dill, parsley, lemon peel and white pepper.

3 Pour milk mixture over noodles. Sprinkle with cheese; toss to coat evenly. Garnish with lemon slices and dill sprigs, if desired. Serve immediately.

Makes 6 (½-cup) servings

Nutrients per Serving:

Calories	173
(18% of calories from fat)	
Total Fat	3 g
Saturated Fat	1 g
Cholesterol	7 mg
Sodium	110 mg
Carbohydrate	27 g
Dietary Fiber	2 g
Protein	8 g
Calcium	104 mg
Iron	1 mg
Vitamin A	51 RE
Vitamin C	6 mg

DIETARY EXCHANGES:
1½ Starch/Bread, ½ Lean Meat, ½ Fat

TOASTED SESAME ORZO

Iron, found in spinach, is needed by the body to aid in the proper function of the immune system and in the production of connective tissue.

1 tablespoon sesame seeds
⅔ cup uncooked orzo pasta
1 teaspoon reduced calorie margarine
1½ cups fresh spinach, washed and coarsely chopped
1 clove garlic, minced
3 tablespoons skim milk
2 tablespoons grated Parmesan cheese
1½ teaspoons fresh oregano *or* ½ teaspoon dried oregano leaves
½ teaspoon paprika
¼ teaspoon ground black pepper

1 Place sesame seeds in small skillet. Cook over medium heat until light golden, stirring constantly. Set aside.

2 Cook pasta according to package directions, omitting salt. Drain and set aside.

3 Melt margarine in medium skillet. Add spinach and garlic; cook over medium heat until spinach is wilted. Stir in milk, cheese, oregano, paprika, black pepper and pasta. Cook over low heat until heated through. Sprinkle with sesame seeds; serve immediately.

Makes 5 (½-cup) servings

Nutrients per Serving:

Calories	116
(19% of calories from fat)	
Total Fat	2 g
Saturated Fat	1 g
Cholesterol	2 mg
Sodium	72 mg
Carbohydrate	19 g
Dietary Fiber	1 g
Protein	5 g
Calcium	68 mg
Iron	1 mg
Vitamin A	110 RE
Vitamin C	4 mg

DIETARY EXCHANGES:
1 Starch/Bread, ½ Fat, 1 Vegetable

Cook's Tip

Mildly sweet, nutty-tasting sesame seeds are commonly found in supermarket spice aisles. Because of their high oil content, sesame seeds can go rancid if kept for long at room temperature. For best results store them in the refrigerator or freezer.

SOUTHERN GREENS AND PASTA

If you are unfamiliar with chicory's bitter-tasting leaves, then you may want to try the more subtle, yet still pungent mustard greens.

Nutrients per Serving:

Calories	88
(13% of calories from fat)	
Total Fat	1 g
Saturated Fat	<1 g
Cholesterol	0 mg
Sodium	39 mg
Carbohydrate	15 g
Dietary Fiber	3 g
Protein	4 g
Calcium	31 mg
Iron	1 mg
Vitamin A	80 RE
Vitamin C	24 mg

DIETARY EXCHANGES:
1 Starch/Bread,
½ Vegetable

2 teaspoons olive oil
1 cup chopped green bell pepper
½ cup chopped onion
½ cup peeled and chopped jicama
⅓ cup chopped celery
1 clove garlic, minced
1 can (14 ounces) ⅓-less-salt chicken broth
2 tablespoons tomato paste
1 teaspoon dried oregano leaves
¼ teaspoon ground black pepper
1 package (10 ounces) frozen black-eyed peas
4 ounces uncooked radiatore or other medium pasta
1 head chicory, mustard greens or kale, washed, ribs removed, thinly sliced
2 to 3 drops red pepper sauce

1 Heat oil in large saucepan over medium heat. Add bell pepper, onion, jicama, celery and garlic. Cook and stir 3 minutes. Stir in chicken broth, tomato paste, oregano and black pepper. Bring to a boil; stir in black-eyed peas. Cover and simmer over low heat 20 minutes or until peas are tender.

2 Cook pasta according to package directions, omitting salt. Drain and set aside.

3 Add chicory to saucepan; cover and cook over low heat until wilted, about 3 minutes. Stir in pasta. Cook until heated through. Season to taste with red pepper sauce. Garnish as desired.   *Makes 12 (½-cup) servings*

TEX-MEX NOODLE CAKE

Noodle cakes are typically Oriental, but try this Tex-Mex version using angel hair pasta and you will insist it comes from the southwest!

Nutrients per Serving:

Calories	183
(20% of calories from fat)	
Total Fat	4 g
Saturated Fat	<1 g
Cholesterol	36 mg
Sodium	136 mg
Carbohydrate	27 g
Dietary Fiber	2 g
Protein	9 g
Calcium	23 mg
Iron	2 mg
Vitamin A	67 RE
Vitamin C	18 mg

DIETARY EXCHANGES:
2 Starch/Bread, ½ Lean
Meat, ½ Fat

8 ounces uncooked angel hair pasta
½ cup finely chopped red bell pepper
1 whole egg plus 1 egg white
3 tablespoons grated Asiago or Parmesan cheese
2 tablespoons skim milk
2 teaspoons chili powder
½ teaspoon cumin
¼ teaspoon ground black pepper
   Plain nonfat yogurt
   Minced fresh cilantro

1 Cook pasta according to package directions, omitting salt. Drain and cool slightly, but do not rinse. Place pasta in medium bowl with bell pepper.

2 Combine whole egg, egg white, cheese, milk, chili powder, cumin and black pepper in small bowl; pour over pasta, tossing to coat evenly.

3 Spray large nonstick skillet with nonstick cooking spray. Add pasta mixture, spreading evenly and pressing firmly. Cook over medium-low heat until bottom is golden brown, about 7 to 8 minutes.

4 Slide noodle cake onto large plate, invert and return noodle cake to skillet. Cook until brown, 3 to 5 minutes.

5 Cut into wedges; serve warm, topped with yogurt and cilantro.

Makes 6 servings

PESTO-PASTA STUFFED TOMATOES

This makes a wonderfully light accompaniment to any chicken or fish entrée.

Nutrients per Serving:

Calories	155
(33% of calories from fat)	
Total Fat	6 g
Saturated Fat	1 g
Cholesterol	2 mg
Sodium	154 mg
Carbohydrate	22 g
Dietary Fiber	3 g
Protein	6 g
Calcium	66 mg
Iron	1 mg
Vitamin A	195 RE
Vitamin C	27 mg

DIETARY EXCHANGES:
1 Starch/Bread, 1 Fat,
1½ Vegetable

3 ounces uncooked star or other small pasta
4 large tomatoes
1 cup loosely packed fresh basil
1 clove garlic, minced
3 tablespoons reduced calorie mayonnaise
1 tablespoon skim milk
¼ teaspoon ground black pepper
1 cup shredded zucchini
4 teaspoons grated Parmesan cheese

1 Cook pasta according to package directions, omitting salt. Drain and rinse; set aside.

2 Cut tops from tomatoes. Scoop out and discard all but ½ cup tomato pulp. Chop tomato pulp and add to pasta. Place tomatoes, cut side down, on paper towels; let drain 5 minutes.

3 Preheat oven to 350°F.

4 Place basil and garlic in blender or food processor; process until finely chopped. Add mayonnaise, milk and black pepper. Process until smooth.

5 Combine pasta mixture, zucchini and basil mixture; toss to coat evenly. Place tomatoes, cut side up, in 8-inch baking dish. Divide pasta mixture evenly among tomatoes, mounding filling slightly. Sprinkle with cheese.

6 Bake 10 to 15 minutes or until heated through. *Makes 4 servings*

PASTA WITH ONION AND GOAT CHEESE

Besides cows, goats also provide milk, which is usually made into goat cheese. This cheese tends to be lower in fat than regular cheeses. It delivers a delightfully tart flavor that easily distinguishes it from other cheeses.

2 teaspoons olive oil
4 cups thinly sliced sweet onions
3 ounces goat cheese
¼ cup skim milk
6 ounces uncooked baby bow tie or other small pasta
1 clove garlic, minced
2 tablespoons dry white wine *or* ⅓-less-salt chicken broth
1½ teaspoons chopped fresh sage *or* ½ teaspoon dried sage leaves
½ teaspoon salt
¼ teaspoon black pepper
2 tablespoons chopped toasted walnuts

1 Heat oil in large nonstick skillet over medium heat. Add onions and cook slowly until golden and caramelized, about 20 to 25 minutes; stir occasionally.

2 Combine goat cheese and milk in small bowl; mix until well blended. Set aside.

3 Cook pasta according to package directions, omitting salt. Drain and set aside.

4 Add garlic to onions in skillet; cook until softened, about 3 minutes. Add wine, sage, salt and black pepper; cook until moisture is evaporated. Remove from heat; add pasta and goat cheese mixture, stirring to melt cheese. Sprinkle with walnuts.

Makes 8 (½-cup) servings

Nutrients per Serving:

Calories	150
(28% of calories from fat)	
Total Fat	5 g
Saturated Fat	<1 g
Cholesterol	9 mg
Sodium	107 mg
Carbohydrate	21 g
Dietary Fiber	2 g
Protein	5 g
Calcium	34 mg
Iron	1 mg
Vitamin A	18 RE
Vitamin C	5 mg

DIETARY EXCHANGES:
1 Starch/Bread, 1 Fat,
1 Vegetable

Personalized Nutrition Reference for Different Calorie Levels*

Daily Calorie Level	1,600	2,000	2,200	2,800
Total Fat	53 g	65 g	73 g	93 g
% of Calories from Fat	30%	30%	30%	30%
Saturated Fat	18 g	20 g	24 g	31 g
Carbohydrate	240 g	300 g	330 g	420 g
Protein	46 g**	50 g	55 g	70 g
Dietary Fiber	20 g***	25 g	25 g	32 g
Cholesterol	300 mg	300 mg	300 mg	300 mg
Sodium	2,400 mg	2,400 mg	2,400 mg	2,400 mg
Calcium	1,000 mg	1,000 mg	1,000 mg	1,000 mg
Iron	18 mg	18 mg	18 mg	18 mg
Vitamin A	1,000 RE	1,000 RE	1,000 RE	1,000 RE
Vitamin C	60 mg	60 mg	60 mg	60 mg

   * Numbers may be rounded
  ** 46 g is the minimum amount of protein recommended for all
     calorie levels below 1,800.
*** 20 g is the minimum amount of fiber recommended for all calorie
     levels below 2,000.

Note: These calorie levels may not apply to children or adolescents, who have varying calorie requirements. For specific advice concerning calorie levels, please consult a registered dietitian, qualified health professional or pediatrician.

Beans
Garbanzo Pasta Salad, 26
Jambalaya, 60
Santa Fe Fusilli, 72
Smoked Turkey Pasta Salad, 20
Southern Greens and Pasta, 84
Spicy Lentil and Pasta Soup, 34
Beef
Fajita Stuffed Shells, 58
Korean-Style Beef and Pasta, 45
Orange Beef and Broccoli, 70
Thai Beef Noodles, 78
Broccoli
Chicken Noodle Roll-Ups, 68
Orange Beef and Broccoli, 70
Pasta Primavera, 56
Sweet and Sour Broccoli Pasta Salad, 18
Vegetable Lasagna, 42

Cheese Tortellini with Tuna, 48
Chicken
Chicken Caesar Salad, 16
Chicken Chow Mein, 62
Chicken Noodle Roll-Ups, 68
Hot Chinese Chicken Salad, 24
Jambalaya, 60
Pad Thai, 50
Plum Chicken, 74
Vegetable-Chicken Noodle Soup, 28
Corn
Easy Tex-Mex Bake, 54
Ginger Wonton Soup, 36
Santa Fe Fusilli, 72

Double Spinach Bake, 64

Easy Tex-Mex Bake, 54
Enlightened Macaroni and Cheese, 66

Fajita Stuffed Shells, 58
Fish
Cheese Tortellini with Tuna, 48
Mediterranean Fish Soup, 38
Salmon and Green Bean Salad with Pasta, 10

Garbanzo Pasta Salad, 26
Gazpacho Macaroni Salad, 14
Ginger Wonton Soup, 36
Green Chile Soup with Spicy Baked Wontons, 30
Grilled Ratatouille, 22

Hot Chinese Chicken Salad, 24

Jamaican Seafood Salad, 12
Jambalaya, 60
Japanese Noodle Soup, 32

Korean-Style Beef and Pasta, 45
Korean-Style Dressing, 46

Lamb; Pastitso, 76
Lasagna, Vegetable, 42
Lemon Tossed Linguine, 80

Mediterranean Fish Soup, 38

Orange Beef and Broccoli, 70

Pad Thai, 50
Pasta Primavera, 56
Pasta with Onion and Goat Cheese, 90
Pastitso, 76
Peas; Straw and Hay, 40
Pesto-Pasta Stuffed Tomatoes, 88
Plum Chicken, 74

Salad Dressings
Korean-Style Dressing, 46
Salads
Chicken Caesar Salad, 16
Garbanzo Pasta Salad, 26
Gazpacho Macaroni Salad, 14
Grilled Ratatouille, 22
Hot Chinese Chicken Salad, 24
Jamaican Seafood Salad, 12
Salmon and Green Bean Salad with Pasta, 10
Smoked Turkey Pasta Salad, 20
Sweet and Sour Broccoli Pasta Salad, 18

Salmon and Green Bean Salad with Pasta, 10
Santa Fe Fusilli, 72
Sauce, Tomato, 44
Shrimp
Jamaican Seafood Salad, 12
Mediterranean Fish Soup, 38
Pad Thai, 50
Side Dishes
Lemon Tossed Linguine, 80
Pasta with Onion and Goat Cheese, 90
Pesto-Pasta Stuffed Tomatoes, 88
Southern Greens and Pasta, 84
Tex-Mex Noodle Cake, 86
Toasted Sesame Orzo, 82
Smoked Turkey Pasta Salad, 20
Soups
Ginger Wonton Soup, 36
Green Chile Soup with Spicy Baked Wontons, 30
Japanese Noodle Soup, 32
Mediterranean Fish Soup, 38
Spicy Lentil and Pasta Soup, 34
Vegetable-Chicken Noodle Soup, 28
Southern Greens and Pasta, 84
Spicy Lentil and Pasta Soup, 34
Spinach
Double Spinach Bake, 64
Toasted Sesame Orzo, 82
Vegetable Lasagna, 42
Straw and Hay, 40
Sweet and Sour Broccoli Pasta Salad, 18
Sweet Potato Ravioli with Asiago Cheese Sauce, 52

Tex-Mex Noodle Cake, 86
Thai Beef Noodles, 78
Toasted Sesame Orzo, 82
Tomato Sauce, 44
Turkey
Easy Tex-Mex Bake, 54
Smoked Turkey Pasta Salad, 20

Vegetable-Chicken Noodle Soup, 28
Vegetable Lasagna, 42

VOLUME MEASUREMENTS (dry)

½ teaspoon = 0.5 mL
¼ teaspoon = 1 mL
½ teaspoon = 2 mL
¾ teaspoon = 4 mL
1 teaspoon = 5 mL
1 tablespoon = 15 mL
2 tablespoons = 30 mL
¼ cup = 60 mL
⅓ cup = 75 mL
½ cup = 125 mL
⅔ cup = 150 mL
¾ cup = 175 mL
1 cup = 250 mL
2 cups = 1 pint = 500 mL
3 cups = 750 mL
4 cups = 1 quart = 1 L

VOLUME MEASUREMENTS (fluid)

1 fluid ounce (2 tablespoons) = 30 mL
4 fluid ounces (½ cup) = 125 mL
8 fluid ounces (1 cup) = 250 mL
12 fluid ounces (1½ cups) = 375 mL
16 fluid ounces (2 cups) = 500 mL

WEIGHTS (mass)

½ ounce = 15 g
1 ounce = 30 g
3 ounces = 90 g
4 ounces = 120 g
8 ounces = 225 g
12 ounces = 360 g
16 ounces = 1 pound = 450 g

DIMENSIONS

1/16 inch = 2 mm
⅛ inch = 3 mm
¼ inch = 6 mm
½ inch = 1.5 cm
¾ inch = 2 cm
1 inch = 2.5 cm

OVEN TEMPERATURES

250°F = 120°C
275°F = 140°C
300°F = 150°C
325°F = 160°C
350°F = 180°C
375°F = 190°C
400°F = 200°C
425°F = 220°C
450°F = 230°C

BAKING PAN SIZES

Utensil	Size in Inches/Quarts	Metric Volume	Size in Centimeters
Baking or	8×8×2	2 L	20×20×5
Cake pan	9×9×2	2.5 L	22×22×5
(square or	12×8×2	3 L	30×20×5
rectangular)	13×9×2	3.5 L	33×23×5
Loaf Pan	8×4×3	1.5 L	20×10×7
	9×5×3	2 L	23×13×7
Round Layer	8×1½	1.2 L	20×4
Cake Pan	9×1½	1.5 L	23×4
Pie Plate	8×1¼	750 mL	20×3
	9×1¼	1 L	23×3
Baking Dish	1 quart	1 L	—
or Casserole	1½ quart	1.5 L	—
	2 quart	2 L	—